A New True Book

TRAINS

By Ray Broekel

This "true book" was prepared
under the direction of
Illa Podendorf,
formerly with the Laboratory School,
University of Chicago

CHILDRENS PRESS, CHICAGO

The author thanks the many railroads he's been able to ride and observe over the years.

Freight train at Sullivan's Curve, Cajon Pass, California

PHOTO CREDITS

Santa Fe Railway Company—Cover, 2, 7, 8, 9, 11, 12 (2 photos), 19, 20 (top right and left), 21 (3 photos), 22, 24, 26, 28, 30, 32, 35, 36, 38, 41.
ICG: Illinois Central Gulf Railroad—18
Amtrak: National Railroad Passenger Corp.—4, 6, 13, 19 (right), 20 (bottom)
Chicago & Northwestern Transit Company—14, 15, 17
Washington Metropolitan Area Transit Authority—43
CTA: Chicago Transit Authority—42 (2 photos)
Seattle-King County Convention & Visitors Bureau—44
COVER—Cyrus K. Holliday and Bicentennial Unit

Library of Congress Cataloging in Publication Data

Broekel, Ray.
   Trains.

   (A New true book)
   Summary: An elementary introduction to trains, what they do, train workers, and kinds of railroad cars.
   1. Railroads—Juvenile literature. [1. Railroads]
I. Title.
TF148.B73   625.1   81-7668
ISBN 0-516-01652-0   AACR2

TABLE OF CONTENTS

Passenger train

THE TRAIN

There it is coming down the track.

It is the train!

The engine is pulling lots of cars.

Now the train is in the station.

All aboard!

Superliner Coach

What are trains?
Trains are a kind of
transportation. Trains carry
passengers.

Freight train crossing Sibley Bridge, Missouri

Trains carry freight.
An engine on wheels
pulls a train. The engine is
called a locomotive.

A train moves on a track.

The track has rails. The rails are made of smooth steel girders.

The rails are laid on ties.
Ties are heavy pieces of
wood. The ties and rails
are on a roadbed.

ENGINES

Train engines are called locomotives. They were first powered by steam. Puffs of used steam came from the smoke stacks.

Very few steam locomotives are still in use today.

Most trains are now
pulled by diesel engines.
And some trains run on
electric power.

PASSENGER TRAINS

Train riders are called
passengers.
Some passengers ride
trains to take long trips.

Other people ride trains
to go to work. These trains
are called commuter trains.

They are used near big
cities.

Many people ride
commuter trains.

They take them to work.

Then they ride them back home.

Some commuter trains are double-deckers. A double-decker car can carry many more passengers.

Trains for long trips carry special cars.

People can sleep on some cars. They are called pullmans.

For food, passengers go to dining cars.

To see the country, people get seats in dome cars.

TRAIN STATIONS

Train stations are called terminals.

People buy tickets at terminals.

They get timetables at them. A timetable tells when different trains stop at and leave a station.

Engineer

Conductor

TRAIN WORKERS

Who are some train
workers we see?

- Engineers
- Brakemen
- Conductors

- Porters
- Ticket sellers
- Roadbed workers

Workers pick up a rail

Welder and helper

Porter

Above: Switchman on diesel engine
Right top: Yardmaster
Right bottom: Computer operator
with a printout

Who are some of the train workers we don't see?

- Switchmen
- Secretaries
- Computer operators
- Mechanics

Train with diesel engine near Flagstaff, Arizona

FREIGHT TRAINS

Most trains are freight trains.

Freight trains carry goods. They carry all kinds of things people use.

There are many kinds of freight cars. Each kind carries different goods.

A boxcar is covered. It carries goods that need to be kept dry.

Some goods need to be
kept cold. They are put in
a refrigerator car.

Freight train with empty gondolas in Abo Canyon, New Mexico

A gondola car has sides but no roof. It carries things that do not need to be kept dry.

Hopper cars are open, too. They carry coal and sand.

98425
98 GALS.

Santa Fe

ATSF 98425

Santa Fe

Santa Fe

Tank cars carry liquids. Some carry oil. Some carry gas. Some carry liquid chocolate. Other liquids are carried, too.

Flatcars have no sides.
Logs can be carried on
them.

35

Some flatcars carry trailers. They are called piggyback flatcars.

A freight train has two ends.

The engine is at the front end.

What brings up the rear?

The caboose. The caboose is an office for the train workers.

SOME SPECIAL TRAINS

All trains run on tracks.
Most tracks are on the
ground.

But some are high
above the ground. Trains
that run on them are
called elevated trains. They
are also called "els."

Some trains run under the ground. They run through tunnels. Such trains are called subways. Subways are found in big cities.

Some trains run on just
one rail. They are called
monorail trains.

One kind of monorail
runs on top of the rail.

Another kind hangs from the rail.

Real trains do work for us.

But some trains are fun to play with, too. They are toy trains. Many boys and girls play with them. And so do lots of grown-ups.

WORDS YOU SHOULD KNOW

aboard (uh • BORD) —to get into a train, ship, or airplane

boxcar —a car of a freight train that is closed on all sides

brakemen — a person who operates the brakes on a train

caboose (kuh • BOOSS) —the last car of a freight train

commute (kuh • MYOOT) —to travel to and from a place

computer operator (kum • PYEW • ter OP • er • ay • ter) —a person who works with computers

conducter (kun • DUK • ter) —the person who collects train tickets

diesel (DEE • sel) —an engine that runs on oil

dining car (DY • ning car) —a car on a train where food is served

dome (DOHM) —a train car with a rounded roof

double-decker (DUB • ul-DEK • er) —one on top of another

electric power (ee • LEK • trik POW • er) —to operate with electricity

electricity (EE • lek • TRISS • uh • tee) —a form of energy that flows through wires

elevated (EL • uh • vay • ted) —a train that runs on rails built above the ground. El is an abbreviation for elevated

engine (EN • jin) —a machine that runs something; locomotive

engineer (en • jin • EER) —a person who runs the engine of a train

freight (FRAYT) —goods; cargo

flatcar —a car of a freight train which is flat and open at the top

girder (GER • der) —a long piece of steel

gondola (GAHN • doh • lah) —a freight car with sides and no top

goods —things that can be bought or sold

hopper —a freight car that can be emptied from the bottom

liquid (LIHK • wid) —a form of matter that is not a solid or a gas; something that flows

locomotive (loh • kuh • MOH • tiv) —the engine of a train

log —a large part of a tree; a trunk of a tree

mechanic (mih • KAN • ik)—a person who can make, use, or repair machines

monorail (MAHN • oh • rayl)—one rail; a train that runs on one rail

passenger (PAS • en • jer)—a person who rides in a train, airplane, bus, car, or ship

piggyback (PIG • ee • bak)—a freight car that carries trailers

porter (POR • ter)—a person who carries luggage and helps passengers

power—to run or operate

puff—a short, quick blow of smoke, air, or steam

pullman—a car on a train which has rooms for sleeping

rail (RAYL)—part of a train track

refrigerator (ree • FRIJ • er • ay • ter)—a car of a freight train which can be kept cold

roadbed—the layer on which railroad ties and tracks are put

secretary (SEK • ruh • tayr • ee)—a person who works in an office and writes letter and keeps records

stack—a chimney

station (STAY • shun)—terminal; a place where a train stops

steel—strong metal

subway—a train that runs underground

switchmen—persons who move sections of train tracks so trains can move from one track to another

terminal (TER • mih • nul)—a train station

tie—a heavy piece of wood to which tracks are attached

timetable (TIME • tay • bul)—a chart which lists the times a train will stop and leave a station

track—the rails on which a train runs

trailer (TRAY • ler)—a large van used to carry goods pulled by a truck

transportation (trans • pohr • TAY • shun)—a way of moving people or goods

trip—a journey; vacation; to travel

tunnel—an underground passage

INDEX

About the Author

Ray Broekel is a full-time freelance writer who lives with his wife, Peg, and a dog, Fergus, in Ipswich, Massachusetts. He has had twenty years of experience as a children's book editor and newspaper supervisor, and has taught many subjects in kindergarten through college levels. Dr. Broekel has had over 1,000 stories and articles published, and over 100 books. His first book was published in 1956 by Childrens Press.